D1798189

1 MONTH OF
FREE
READING

at

www.ForgottenBooks.com

By purchasing this book you are eligible for one month membership to ForgottenBooks.com, giving you unlimited access to our entire collection of over 1,000,000 titles via our web site and mobile apps.

To claim your free month visit:
www.forgottenbooks.com/free890189

ISBN 978-0-266-79290-1
PIBN 10890189

The Dundee Market Crosses & Tolbooths

With Views of New & Old Dundee

Published for Private Circulation

With William Kidd's Compliments

Palace Buildings
Whitehall Street
Dundee

PUBLISHER'S NOTE.

WILLIAM KIDD most gratefully thanks his numerous friends and customers for their kind and liberal patronage for the past thirty years, during which he has carried on business on his own account ; and asks them to honour him by accepting this Brochure in remembrance of the completion of his business-life of a half-century, which began with his apprenticeship to the bookselling and stationery trade under the late Mr Frederick Shaw. He trusts they will find the little book both entertaining and interesting, and also appreciate his humble effort, in this form, to excite in Dundonians of the present generation a desire to make themselves acquainted with the early history of their native city, and to help older citizens to preserve their remembrance of it. At first it was intended to present a succinct History of the Market Crosses and Tolbooths only, but subsequent reflection resulted in a decision to accompany it with a paper published about 1830, entitled " Reminiscences of the Days of Old," and to provide three other historical sketches relating to the city as it was sixty years ago—all of which, it is believed, will be read with lively interest.

A NEW BOOK ON DUNDEE.

W. K. has in the Press " A History of Ancient Dundee " (oblong 4to.), which will be issued in a few months. Its preparation has occupied a very long time, the object being to secure accuracy and comprehensiveness. It contains a History of Ancient Dundee, Articles on Dundee as it existed at different periods, History of the Spinning Trade, Mr T. Y. Miller's History of the Printing Trade, and numerous ancient and modern views. W. K. also gratefully acknowledges his indebtedness to Mr T. Y. Miller, Mr J. S. Neish, and Mr Alexander Hutcheson, for kind assistance, and to Mr Alexander Wilson and Mr William Bertie for photographs.

WHITEHALL STREET,
DUNDEE, 1901.

OLD MURRAYGATE.

Trades' Hall and Narrow of Murraygate—all demolished to widen the street.

NEW MURRAYGATE.

Photo. from a Sketch

by Mr D. L. Anderson.

CONTENTS.

LIST OF ILLUSTRATIONS.

THE CHURCH TOWER.   *Photo by Mr W. Bertie.*

The Executive, of which a reduced copy is here presented, was painted by Henry Harwood about 1821. It is a representation of the leading men in the Dundee Town Council, and other noted citizens, who have gathered at mid-day on the High Street, as was their wont, to discuss and settle public affairs. The sketches are generally broad even to caricature, but they are full of character and humour, and were considered good likenesses of the familiar features of municipal rulers. Henry Harwood died in 1868, at the age of 65, and was buried in the Eastern Necropolis.

1. Justice Blair, Cloth Inspector (*Faculty*).
2. Thomas Bell, Manufacturer, Provost from 1828 to 1831.
3. Patrick Anderson, Provost from 1818 to 1823 (*The Previous Question*).
4. David Brown, Clothier, was twice Provost of Dundee (*Rise to order*).
5. Bailie Reid, Merchant (*The Powerful Executive*).
6. George Rough, Glover (*Interdict, or the Man of Breeches*).
7. Rev. James Thomson, 50 years Minister of the Steeple Church (*The Powers that be*).
8. Robert Christie, Shipping Agent, Coal Merchant, &c. (*Protests Ready Made*).
9. Deacon Cathro, Dyer (*Set the Mills, or No. 9 has it*).
10. Samuel Addison, Deacon of the Flesher Incorporation (*Corporation in hand*).
11. John How, Bootmaker, High Street (*A Potsherd*).
12. Thomas Spalding, Manufacturer (*Not Competent*).
13. John Baxter, Writer (*Judas*).
14. Walter Thomson, Shoemaker (*Ishmael, or the Solicitor's Jackall*).
15. Robert Mudie, Teacher, and Editor of "Advertiser" (*The Highest Bidder*).
16. George Clark, Shipowner (*Go Between*).

THE EXECUTIVE.

THE

DUNDEE MARKET CROSSES

AND TOLBOOTHS.

THEIR HISTORY AND ASSOCIATIONS.

WHEN EDWARD VII. was proclaimed King of the British Empire, an idea was entertained by many of the citizens of Dundee that the ceremony should have been performed on, or near, the circle in the causeway, which marks the spot on the High Street where the Cross once stood. The claims of the Old Cross, however, were ignored in favour of a crimson-draped platform erected in front of the Town House. That incident, nevertheless, awakened an interest in the Cross, and evoked a desire to know something concerning its history and traditions. Every one who takes an interest in the City wherein he dwells ought to acquaint himself with its history. With the object, therefore, of spreading knowledge of our local history, the following pages have been written.

In ancient times it was the prevailing custom to erect a Cross, the symbol of the Christian faith, by waysides and in the centre of towns and villages. The locality of the Cross in Dundee became a favourite resort for the inhabitants, where they could talk over the news of the day, and buy and sell or exchange the products of their industry. Though the symbol of Christ's sufferings and death, had been raised to foster reverence and piety, the open space around it soon degenerated into a rendezvous for gossips and idlers, and became the scene of daily or weekly marketing. And so the Town Cross assumed the name of "The Market Cross." Many of those ancient structures may yet be seen in small villages or decayed burgh towns. From most cities of importance they have long been removed, though in several they have been restored as relics of the past, as may be seen in Edinburgh and Dundee. Dundee has had three Crosses, or, rather, the Cross has occupied three different sites in the course of the past seven centuries. Adjoining the Cross, and closely associated with it, was the Tolbooth, a building combining Town House and prison. Thus the symbols of law and social order were planted in the very heart of the community.

The Tolbooth and Cross of Dundee were first erected in the Seagate. These institutions were set up in that street about the middle of the thirteenth century; but, as Mr Alex. Maxwell says in his *Old Dundee*, we have no records to show what they were like. The town existed at that time, and perhaps centuries prior to that date, yet there is no history extant to tell us what sort of people dwelt in the town, or how they contrived to exist. The old burgh of Dundee was but a very small town, and the Seagate, or, as it was formerly called, the Highgate, was the principal street. The town was limited to a small area on the flat shore of the Tay, between the Meadows' Burn on the west, and the Dens' Burn on the east. The Meadows' Burn washed the eastern base of the Castle Rock, on a portion of which St. Paul's Episcopal Church and spire are built, while the Dens' Burn entered the river or sea about St. Roque's Lane. St. Mary's Church, in the Nethergate, with its fine square tower, was long known as the "Church in the Field," as there were then no buildings east of the present High Street. Most of the houses in the Seagate were built of wood, and it is probable the first Tolbooth was a timber erection, mean and shabby, but quite in harmony with its squalid surroundings. The site of the first Tolbooth and Cross was opposite the foot of Peter Street, which has just been demolished with the old buildings on the north side for the widening and improving of that old thoroughfare.

OUR LADY WARKSTAIR.

At the west end of the second tolbooth in the High Street stood Lady Warkstair's house—the last of the picturesque old houses of that description. In the Rental Roll of 1581 it is designed—"The land callet our Lady Wark. stayris, and also the tenement called the Lady Wark Stairs lying next at the west end of the tenement callet the Auld Tolbuith."

The house of Our Lady Wark Stair, or as it was anciently designated, Our Lady Wark, had probably at first been an hospital or almshouse endowed for the maintenance of indigent women, and piously dedicated to the Virgin. In 1548, along with many other houses, it was burned by the English invaders, and thereafter restored to the condition in which it stood till its recent removal. With its timber-fronted double gable turned outward, its narrow irregular windows and nest of small shops, it continued to be conspicuous among modern buildings as a quaint example of old burghal architecture.

The Vault is a heavy semi-circular archway which formerly opened directly on the haven, and was one of the three accesses to the old harbour. On its south side were gates, which, like the other ports in the burgh, used to be closed at night for the general security. St. Clement's Church stood in the line of the timber-fronted houses on the left, the uppermost of them—the old Weigh-house— having been part of the Church itself. The burying ground extended from Tindal's Wynd westward to where Crichton Street is now. The building, which enters from a small courtyard on the right, was the town house of the Lairds of Strathmartine; and is a very interesting specimen of old burghal architecture. It has a fine entrance and stair, and the principal apartments are panelled in oak. From its erection it has been known as "Strathmartine's Lodging."

PLACE OF OLD ST. CLEMENT'S CHURCH AND STRATHMARTINE'S LODGING, VAULT.

The site of the Cross is marked by a circle of causeway stones. In the improved street that old landmark it is hoped will be retained. It was in the Seagate where Wallace slew the English Governor's son, and thereby drew the sword in the cause of Scotland's national independence. Centuries after Wallace had gone to rest, Grizzel Jaffray was burned, it is said, in the Seagate, for the imaginary crime of witchcraft. As she is said to have been the last witch burned in Dundee, other poor females had doubtless previously fallen a prey to bigotry, and perished at the stake.

The Cross has in the course of its history occupied three different sites. About the beginning of the fifteenth century, the population having increased considerably and the town beginning to extend westwards, the Seagate was abandoned as a market place in favour of a more open space now occupied as the High Street, and the Cross was removed to and re-erected at the west end of that street, opposite the new Tolbooth there and almost opposite the top of Crichton Street. The figure of St. Andrew's Cross, formed of causeway blocks, still marks the second site of the Cross. There is no knowledge as to when the original Tolbooth in the Seagate ceased to be used, but at a later period the Tolbooth, as already mentioned, occupied a site opposite the head of Crichton Street, and between the house of " Our Lady Warkstairs " on the west and the corner land on the east. Part of that site is now occupied by the four-storeyed tenement in which Mr Henry Dixon, ironmonger, has his shop. The second Tolbooth, although much injured by fire when the English burned the town in 1548, continued to be used until 1562, when, a new house having been erected on the south side of the street, it was used for other purposes, and became known as the " Auld Tolbuith." It had been a timber-fronted building, having, along the ground storey a line of wooden or stone pillars which supported the upper structure and formed a piazza in front of the booths—the burghal chambers being probably all above. After its abandonment it is understood to have existed as a public building until it was taken down about, it is under-stood, the end of the eighteenth century. A " large land " of stone, afterwards erected in its place, was named "Camperdown" by the proprietor, in honour of Admiral Duncan's signal victory over the Dutch Fleet at Camperdown, in 1797.

An idea of what the old Tolbooth had been like may be formed from the quaint architecture of a neighbouring building, known as "My Lady Warkstair's House," which was demolished about twelve years ago. On its site was reared a palatial edifice, still known as Lady Warkstair's House, with a fine front elevation embracing two splendid shops. My Lady Warkstairs' was a religious almshouse connected with the Church of the Blessed Virgin (the Nethergate Church) before the Reformation. It was a four-storeyed house, with a couple of quaint gables facing the street, and, judging from the prevailing style in those medieval times, the Tolbooth may have been similar in appearance.

After the lapse of one hundred and forty years it was reported to the Magistrates that the Cross was in a dilapidated and ruinous condition. The stones, which had been brought from the Seagate building, were crumbling away by the action of time and the weather. Accordingly it was decided to erect a new Cross, on a site further east, now indicated on the street by the stone circle, with cross in the centre, a few yards from the foot of Reform Street.

THE MARKET CROSS.

The new Cross was designed by Mr John Mylne, Her Majesty's Master Mason for Scotland. It was an octagonal, ornate structure, surrounded by a base or platform, which was reached by a flight of six steps. There was a door in one of the sides, from which a stair led to the arched battlemented roof. From the centre of the octagonal structure rose a tall, slender stone shaft, surmounted by a unicorn, bearing between its fore feet a shield, on which was a carving of the Scottish Lion. The sculptor placed the lion looking toward the left instead of the right side of the shield. Near the top, on one of the sides of the column, were the lilies of the arms of the city, with the motto, "Dei Donum," and "1586"—the year of its erection. On one of the sides of the pillar may yet be seen the letters I. M. M., the initials of John

THE MARKET CROSS.

The last Market Cross erected on the High Street, opposite the Town House,
by John Mylne, Master Mason of Scotland, removed in 1777.

The Market Cross, which from an early time stood upon the Market Gait, had, by 1582, become ruinous, and another was then erected in its place by John Mylne, a famous mason of the period. It was an octagonal decorated structure, rising from a platform which was reached by an ascent of six steps, and having an arched and battlemented roof, from which rose a stone shaft surmounted by a unicorn bearing a shield on which was the Scottish lion. The cross was the central point in the burgh where proclamations were made and public acts were notified, and it was a usual place for the punishment of offenders. On market days the farmer's wives sat on the steps selling their eggs and butter, and the farmers stood round the place chaffering about their corn. Last century, when the King's birthday came round, the magistrates would get upon the upper platform and there, with accompanying cheers, drink his Majesty's health.

Since the demolition of the Cross in 1777, its stone shaft has remained almost entire, although it narrowly escaped destruction. It was several times put away into corners, and was only saved from being made into paving stones because it was not worth the labour. Happily this pillar has now been erected on a fitting site within the church railings at the foot of Lindsay Street, where it stands a curious memorial of the past.

Mylne, the builder. When the public wells were erected, about the year 1749, to supply the town with water from the Lady-well reservoir at foot of Hilltown, one was placed on the High Street, on the east side of the Cross, and was called the Cross Well. There were eight such wells, and these, erected at convenient parts of the town, gave at the time what was considered an ample water supply for the public. As the population increased, as it did after the beginning of the nineteenth century, the wells became utterly inadequate, and during the long controversy about the introduction of a gravitation supply of one of the most essential elements of life, water was hawked through the streets in carts as milk is sold now.

In bygone days the Cross was the centre of attraction in the town. On market days the farmers' wives sat on the steps around the platform, while the farmers gathered around on the street; the former selling the produce of the dairy and poultry yard, and the latter driving hard bargains with millers and corn merchants. The farmers still continue to meet on the High Street, in spite of Magisterial remonstrances and recommendations, and electric car disturbances. Public proclamations, whether of Municipal or National importance, were made from the battlements of the octagonal structure bearing the Cross. When the King's birthday came round the Provost and Magistrates proceeded from the Tolbooth to the Cross, and on the roof they pledged His Majesty's health in flowing bumpers of wine before the assembled inhabitants. At such joyous and festive seasons the Magistrates generously shared the good cheer with their fellow-townsmen. By some mechanical contrivance gargoyles or ornamental rain-water holes around the bartizan were made to flow with wine or ale to slake the thirst of the " drouthy " crowd. The scramble for " free drinks " would not have been considered conducive to the good moral behaviour of the people in these modern days. Men and women provided themselves with pails, cogs, and such domestic vessels as were then in use, and fought and jostled each other in ascending the steps to catch a drop from the intoxicating stream.

" Pour out the red wine, let it flow
Like a clear and bounding river "

might have been appropriately sung by that eager, seething crowd. These were rude times, and such bacchanalian orgies would-be denounced now both by pulpit and press. The Cross was also the place of public punishment for petty offenders condemned to the jougs, the stocks, or the pillory. Social intercourse, friendship, love, centred round the Market Cross. It was a common meeting place of the inhabitants, and the lovers' trysting spot. Around the Cross, and on the High Street, the inhabitants met in the evening to discuss the news and enjoy a breath of fresh air in the open area after the business and toils of the day. That once popular picture, " The Executive," in the true Hogarth style, drawn by the late Mr Henry Harwood, a local artist of high merit, gives a realistic idea of the scene on the High Street some seventy or eighty years ago.

THE TOWN HOUSE.

" The Town House is built in a hole," remarked a writer in the *Dundee Magazine* in the end of the eighteenth century. That surely was a very undignified situation for so fine a public building. Nevertheless, the writer was perfectly correct. The Market Place, or High Street itself, was in a hollow between two rolling knolls, the Castle Rock on the south east, and a long ridge on the north, extending from Commercial Street on the east to North Tay Street on the west. Castle Street was cut through the Castle, or Black Rock ; and the excavations in Reform Street, Barrack Street, and Lindsay Street have levelled down the rocky ridge on the north. Indeed, the High Street itself was higher in its original state than it appears at the present time. On two occasions at least that fine oblong area had been subjected to cutting down operations till it had been brought to its present level condition. The present Town House was built in 1734 on what was the original site of St. Clement's Parish Church, the ground behind sloping gently down to the shore of the bay that lay between the Castle Rock and St. Nicholas Craig, or the Chapel Rock. Within that basin was the old harbour, now represented by the Greenmarket. St. Clement's

TOWN HOUSE.

Thomas Donaldson's Shop, 1791.

The Town House was built in 1737. The piazza was open only in front, there being a large oblong window at each end, so that those who sat gossiping on the seats within were protected from draughts at the ends. Those windows were long ago converted into open accesses.

was the only original Parish Church of Dundee ; and around it, on the sunny slope overlooking the beautiful river, was the graveyard, where the " Fathers of the Hamlet slept." As the little grave-yard had become too small for the town, Mary Queen of Scots presented the Town Council with the garden and grounds of the old Nunnery, on the north side of the town, as a burying place. St. Clement's grave-yard was, therefore, abandoned, and the "Howff" henceforth became the Town's burying place. The Town House was therefore built on sacred ground. To this day a portion of the old churchyard wall, apparently a pillar of one of the gates, may be seen at the rear of that building, on the east side of the entrance to St. Clement's Lane. The present Town House is the fourth, some authorities say the fifth, Municipal building which Dundee has possessed. There is talk of building a sixth if a good site could be secured. But where ?

At the south side of the entrance of the Overgate stands an old house fronting the High Street, having a flat capped turret at its north-east angle. This building was once connected with the erections used as the Council Chambers after the Town House or Tolbooth in Seagate had been abandoned. It was called the " New Tolbuith " ; and burgh records state that in 1590 a contract was entered into for erecting upon it an octagonal turret for the hang-ing of the Guildry bell. That building subsequently became the property of the Buccleugh family. Within its walls, about 1650, was born Anne, Duchess of Buccleugh, who afterwards, by marriage with the ill-fated Duke of Monmouth, became Duchess of Buc-cleugh and Monmouth. It would appear that the " New Tol-booth " had become unsuitable for the business of the town, for the vestry of St. Clement's Church was obtained for holding the Council meetings. Another Tolbooth was subsequently erected on a strip of ground between the " Muckle Gate " and the wall of St. Clement's graveyard. Little is known of the building; it must have been but a temporary erection to serve the exigencies of the times.

The present Town House was designed by Mr William Adam, the most famous Architect of his time. It is a massive structure, in what is known as the Palladian style of architecture. The

piazza in front with seven arches, popularly known as the
" Pillars," has always been a favourite resort of the citizens.
Originally these " Pillars " were closed at the east and west ends,
and had windows fitted in the arches. The arched roof supports
the floors of the Town Hall and Guild Hall on the first storey.
The upper flats were long used as the common prison. The grand
old building has a rather imposing appearance, which is still
further enhanced by a fine spire, rising to the height of one
hundred and forty feet. Between twenty and thirty years ago
a large addition was made at the rear of the main building. To
make room for these additions some quaint old buildings had to
be demolished. One of these antique structures was a genuine
relic of old Dundee, which it was believed had at one time been
the Grammar and Music School attached to St. Clement's
Church.

DUNDEE AT A LOW EBB.

Considering the condition of the town at the beginning of the
eighteenth century, we cannot but admire the moral courage
and public spirit which inspired the Magistrates and Council, when
they faced the erection of that spacious Town House. Dundee
had fallen on evil times. Its staple trade, the manufacture of
coarse woollen cloth, had been crushed by the Union of Scotland
and England. For centuries the trade had been successfully
prosecuted in the town ; the product of the looms, above what
was required for home consumption, found a ready market on
the Continent, where the cloth was used to make clothing for
soldiers. By a clause in the Treaty of Union the manufacture of
woollen goods was restricted to certain English towns, thereby
creating a monopoly for England, and depriving Scotland of one
of her old established industries.

The first great blow which fell on the town was its siege and
sack by General Monk, on 5th September, 1651. About one-
sixth of the inhabitants were slain in the massacre that followed
the storming of the town, and an immense booty was seized
by the victorious Monk. Prior to that terrible disaster the town
had been very prosperous, and its population, according to the

OLD CUSTOM HOUSE, GREENMARKET.

OLD HOUSES, MURRAYGATE.

estimate of the Rev. Dr Small, parish minister, and author of the Statistical Account of the Parish, must have numbered eleven or twelve thousand. That blow was disastrous, and the Treaty of Union seemed as if it would depopulate the town altogether.

Dundee had then a mean and poverty-stricken appearance. Most of the houses were built of timber or a combination of wood and stone. In the Seagate, the principal street, there were not more than half-a-dozen stone-built houses. According to the late Mr A. C. Lamb, the Seagate began at Tindal's Wynd, and continued eastward to about the locality now known as Sugar House Wynd. With straggling rows of houses, the town did not extend westward beyond Tay Street, Nethergate, and Argyll-gate or Overgate. The houses were not so closely built together as they are now, many of them, even the closes, having gardens attached. The Meal Market was at the west end of the High Street, and the Tron or Weigh-house was in the same locality. At the head of the Murraygate, between that street and the Seagate, the shambles or slaughter-houses were established, and remained there for years. Once a week a Horse-market was held in the narrow of the Murraygate and Seagate, where the animals were raced up and down in those congested thoroughfares to the great danger of the inhabitants. The streets were unpaved, the roadways were full of mud and holes, and street lamps were then unknown, so that it was dangerous to go about after dark.

Yet, withal, Dundee must have been a pleasant place to live in, and well deserved its pet name "Bonnie Dundee." Its situation on the shores of the ever-beautiful Tay gives it a peculiar charm. In those early days the shores presented all the romantic beauty they derived from the hand of Nature. It is not surprising, therefore, that the town was a favourite residence of many of the Scottish nobility, and even of Royalty itself. Near the foot of the Overgate, and at Whitehall Close, in the Nethergate, there stood two palaces, in which several of the Kings of Scotland resided at various times. Mention has already been made of the Buccleugh family residence. That ancient building in Greenmarket, known as the Old Custom House, was the town residence of the Drummond family. Near the junction of Union Street with the Nethergate a quaint old timber mansion stood in the olden times, which was once occupied by the Earls of Crawford, and its garden, situated behind, sloped towards the river. In the Vault, and within a gate opening into a small paved court, was a fine example of old burgh architecture, still known as Strathmartine's Lodgings, being the town residence of that family. The highway running along the shore to St. Nicholas' Craig, known as Fish Street, now occupied by Whitehall Crescent, was once wholly occupied by the houses inhabited by wealthy country gentlemen.

THE FATE OF THE OLD CROSS.

After having stood on the streets of Dundee in at least three different places, the Old Market Cross was finally removed as an obstruction to the thoroughfare. In the year 1777 that quaint structure was demolished. The platform and octagonal tower were carted away as rubbish, the least decayed stones being selected to be used in other buildings. The stone shaft, also, was preserved, and placed beside the Old Steeple. With the demolition of the Cross, the Cross Well was cleared away from the High Street, but, as water was an essential to the people, the well was re-erected behind the Town House in St. Clement's Lane. In that situation it remained for nearly one hundred years, when, being rendered unnecessary by the introduction of the Lintrathen water supply, it was also demolished, along with the old buildings in the Vault and St. Clement's Lane, to make room for the additions to the Town House. The stone shaft or pillar of the old Cross lay in its ignoble and obscure resting place beside the Steeple for many years. Meanwhile the population of Dundee had been increasing by leaps and bounds. With the influx of people—from Ireland, and from the small towns and rural districts of Scotland—who were attracted by the abundance of employment to be found in the mills and factories, crime also increased. The old cells in the upper flats of the Town House became utterly inadequate for the confinement of offenders,

CROSS, NETHERGATE,

Photo. by — Mr Alex. Wilson.

ver.
urt,
ath-

raig,
was
ntry

three
an
aint
tower

was
moli-
the
the
ent's
dred
of the
old
for the
of the
place
ion of
the
rural
e of
also
Town

and part of the Old Steeple had to be utilised as a prison, till "Bridewell" in Bell Street was built. When the Old Steeple was thus degraded into a "lock-up," the shaft of the old Cross was set up at the west door of the Tower. The unicorn was once more fitted on the top of the shaft, and adorned with a new tail. And now the poor old Cross has found a more dignified resting place in the south west corner of the ornamental grounds of the Churches in Nethergate. The shaft stands on a model of the old octagonal structure, with platform and steps in miniature, and there is thus presented to the view of the passer-by that relic of medieval sculpture four hundred years old. When the cross was removed from the High Street an arrangement of the causeway, in the form of an octagonal figure, marked its site and the space it occupied ; the figures 1586 and 1777, cut on the stones, being the respective dates of its erection and removal. When the High Street was lowered, after the opening of Reform Street, the octagonal form was abolished, and the site marked by a disposition of the stones showing a cross in the centre of a circle, which are preserved to the present day, and will, in all likelihood, continue to all generations.

ST. CLEMENT'S MANSE & OLD GRAMMAR SCHOOL.

12

MONK AND THE "NEW TOLBUITH."

(See page 7).

THE SIEGE AND SACK OF DUNDEE.

IN other respects the "New Tolbuith"—the old building at
the south-east corner of Overgate, which has recently undergone extensive structural alterations—may well take rank as one
of the historic relics that time has left within the city. It is
believed that it was in this old house General Monk took up his
quarters after he had beseiged and captured the town. During his
residence there he was stricken with a fever and lay for weeks at
the point of death. That illness and other calamties which over·
took him were regarded as a Divine judgment against him,
because of the atrocities he had perpetrated on the inhabitants.

The siege of Dundee, and the massacre of the inhabitants, by
General Monk have in some degree tarnished the military glory
of the great soldier who so nobly acquitted himself as the leader
of the Parliamentary Army in the Great Civil War. The people
of Dundee rendered themselves obnoxious to Cromwell and his
party by their adherence to the Solemn League and Covenant.
When Charles I. threatened to introduce Prelacy into Scotland
the nation revived the Covenant in opposition to the blind policy
of that self-willed monarch. The deed was signed in Greyfriars
Churchyard, Edinburgh, by nearly all the nobility and common
people, some even writing their names with their own blood.
Among others who subscribed the deed was the Marquis of Montrose, but when the war broke out Montrose abjured the Covenant and took up arms in defence of the King. During those
troublous times Dundee was twice besieged : first by Montrose,
and afterwards by Monk.

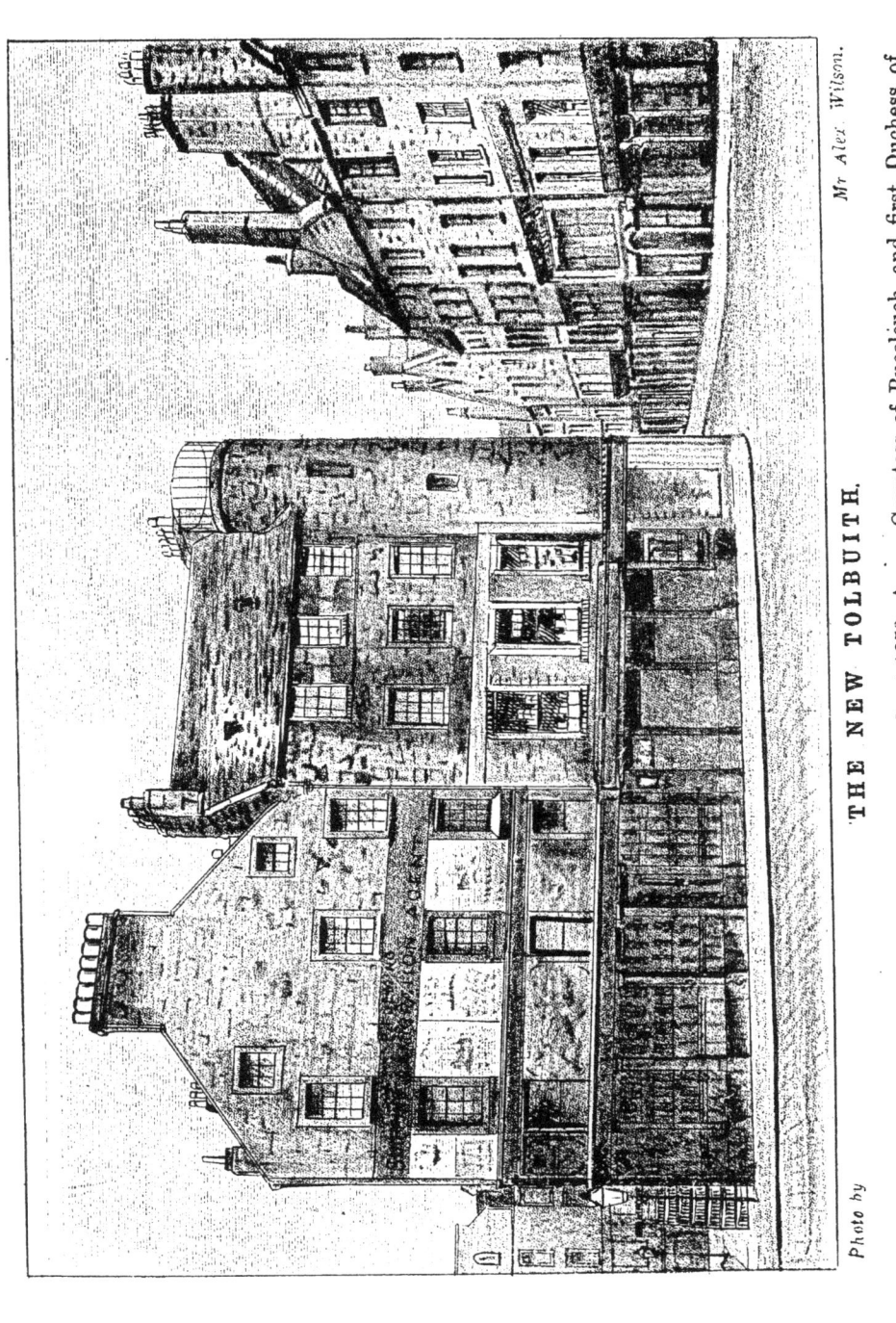

Photo by   Mr Alex Wilson.

THE NEW TOLBUITH.

In this, one of the old Tolbooths, was born, about 1650, Anne, Countess of Buccleuch, and first Duchess of Buccleuch and Monmouth. When General Monk stormed the town on 1st September, 1651, he took up his quarters in this house, and being smitten with a fever, he lay there very ill for many weeks.

"The Luckenbooths."

A quaint bit of the old High Street is yet to be found at the bottom of the Overgate, in the building designated from the time of its erection, "The Luckenbooths." The shops or booths in the old burgh used to be open to the street, similar to some that were left, still within the memory of many people yet alive, in the Narrow of the Murraygate. About two hundred and fifty years ago, enclosed or locked booths began to be made ; and this, as probably the first building in which the improvement was introduced, became known by that name. The floors are of higher elevation than was then usual, and at the corner there is a turret stair which rises above the roof and is surrounded by a rail. In 1650, this house was the residence of the Earl of Buccleuch, and here his daughter Anne, who became the wife of the Duke of Monmouth, the unfortunate son of Charles II., was born. During the subsequent occupation of the town by the English, General Monk is said to have lived in it.

13

Montrose appeared with his army and encamped on the heights of Clatto, whence he made a sudden descent with a portion of his army on the town on the morning of 4th April, 1645, and demanded the governor to surrender. No answer was returned at first, the object of the governor being to gain time, in order to obtain assistance. But Montrose would brook no delay. He stormed the walls at three places simultaneously. A vigorous defence was maintained by the besieged, but the enemy seized the guns and turned their fire on the town. They captured the Church and the Market Place, and set fire to some of the houses. The wild Highlanders and Irish, of which Montrose's army was composed, took to pillage as usual; while the looting and burning were in progress Montrose stood on a hill in the centre of the town and viewed the scene with complacency. But Baillie and Hurry, commanding the Covenanters, crossed the Tay with three thousand men, and Montrose had to collect his scattered troops and retreat from the town in hot haste.

The siege of Dundee by General Monk was the most serious disaster that ever befel the town. Six years had passed away and brought about a change in the political situation. Charles I. had been executed, and the Commonwealth, with Oliver Cromwell as Protector, had been set up. The Scottish people still held to the Solemn League and Covenant, and opposed Cromwell. Charles II. was invited to come to Scotland, and assistance was promised to enable him to regain the throne. He arrived in Dundee, where he was entertained by the Magistrates and the landed gentry. Charles, ready to do anything to gain the throne, signed the Covenant, and was duly crowned at Scone. Dundee supplied Charles with men and money, and the army under General Leslie was ready to fight for their young king.

Cromwell marched into Scotland to suppress this new phase of the war. At Dunbar he defeated Leslie; then marching northward he captured Leith and Edinburgh, crossed the Forth reduced Stirling, and seized Perth. Dundee had been marked out by Cromwell and Monk for special vengeance. That town was the last stronghold of the Royalists and had to be seized.

Meanwhile Leslie, after his defeat at Dunbar, retreated to Falkirk, where he was joined by the King. The army having been strongly reinforced, Leslie marched south and invaded England. By that bold manœvure he got in rear of Cromwell, and threatened to cut his communications. On receiving intelligence of Leslie's stratagem Cromwell with the bulk of his army immediately set off in pursuit, leaving Monk to besiege Dundee. Cromwell overtook the Royalists at Worcester, where he defeated them, the King narrowly escaping capture by the Roundheads. Monk lost no time in carrying out his plans. He appeared before Dundee in the end of July 1651, and put his forces in order to commence the siege. He next sent a letter to the Governor, demanding the surrender of the town, which was answered by the following reply :—

"Sir,—We received yours. For answer thereto we acquaint you and all officers and troops that are at present in arms against the King's authority to lay down your arms and come in and join with His Majesty's forces in this kingdom and to continue to give obedience to His Majesty's declaration, sent you herewith, which if you will obey we shall continue, sir, your faithful friend in the old manner.—Robert Lumsden."

Monk considered this an arrogant and insolent answer. The town was accordingly invested and the siege vigorously pressed. But the works had been well strengthened, and the garrison made a stubborn resistance. Weeks passed on, and measures were being concerted to endeavour to relieve the town. A Committee of the Estates assembled at Alyth, and collected a large force to attack Monk and compel him to raise the siege. But Monk had friends in the country as well as in the town—men who were opposed to the King. From these spies, if they might be so called, he received valuable information, which brought him the victory he sought. Having learned of the assembling of troops at Alyth, he despatched his cavalry to surprise and capture them. His troops were guided across the Sidlaws by men well acquainted with the country. The English troops pounced on the Royalists' camp during the night, and captured all the leaders before they could make any show of resistance.

In the meantime Monk had obtained valuable information

THE OLD STEEPLE AS IT IS BELIEVED TO HAVE STOOD ORIGINALLY.

As originally built, the tower was surmounted by stone arches which no doubt, gave it a more imposing apppearance than it now presents. The crowning structure remained entire until 1547, when the English recklessly destroyed it by setting fire to the timber floor underneath. No attempt was made to restore the broken arches overhead, but the material of which they were built was used in the construction of the Pent house which yet surmounts the tower.—*Alex. Maxwell's Old Dundee.*

From a Print.

Photo by Mr W. Bertie

THE OLD STEEPLE AS IT ONCE STOOD—Viewed from the East.

This view of Steeple and Wind Mill is from Pennant's Journey in Scotland, 1772, and was sketched before the present St. Clement's Church was re-built. The Windmill was erected on what was known as the Centre Hill, which covered the present Lindsay Street Quarry.

regarding the condition of the town, which decided him to deliver an assault without waiting for the return of his cavalry. It is said that the spy to whom he was indebted for his information was a Scottish boy, who in sport was in the habit of climbing over the walls in daylight unchallenged by the sentinels. Whether the lad found his way to the English camp voluntarily or as a prisoner history sayeth not. He told Monk that every forenoon the soldiers and strangers—for the town was full of refugees—were in the habit of getting drunk. Old chroniclers tell how it was the practice of the people in Dundee and other towns to breakfast in the alehouses. At a time of such great excitement as a siege they indulged pretty freely, and by midday soldiers and civilians were generally pretty well muddled.

On the first of September Monk stormed the works. The town soldiers, who had been caught napping, obeyed the call to arms promptly, and met the stormers with a stout resistance ; but they had scarcely recovered from their surprise when the enemy, who had entered the town from the west, were pouring through the streets like a flood.

Lumsden, the governor, with a small body of his men retired to the Old Steeple, fighting all the way, and there defended themselves bravely against the strong body of troops that endeavoured to storm the old tower Around the old tower the battle raged fiercely. It was the last stand of the brave defenders, but their enemies were furious and relentless. Finding that they could not force the tower, they resorted to a base expedient, Bundles of wet straw were collected and piled and set on fire around the tower, and the brave fellows were smoked out like a hive of bees. Lumsden and the survivors of his little party surrendered to Capt. Kelly That officer, admiring the gallantry of Lumsden in the defence of the Tower, was conveying him to General Monk to intercede for his life when a Major Butler barbarously shot Lumsden dead. Monk was said to have been greatly grieved at that unfortunate incident. But he had evidently no control over the brutal passions of his soldiers or he would have stayed the massacre of innocent men, women, and children that followed the siege.

In the fight between seven or eight hundred of the garrison

and people fell along with the brave Governor; and one writer
says that two hundred defenceless women and children were
massacred by the riotous victors while pillaging the town.

The spoil which fell to the victors was immense, exceeding in
value two and a half million pounds Scots. At that time all the
wealth of the landed gentry, not only of the district, but of
Fife, Edinburgh, and the Lothians, was stored in Dundee for
safety, embracing gold and silver, silver plate, jewels, and rich
merchandise. Retribution fell on Monk for the atrocities he had
been guilty of. He fell sick of a fever, and lay for months at the
point of death in the " auld tolbuith " at the foot of the Overgate.
Sixty ships were laden with the plunder to be conveyed by sea to
London. The fleet sailed on an October day, but strange to relate
every ship foundered in the Tay within sight of the town, and the
plunder was utterly lost. This disaster was regarded as " the
just judgment of God."

OLD HOUSES, FISH STREET.

DOCKS SEVENTY YEARS AGO

THE OLD LONDON PADDLE STEAMER.

17

REMINISCENCES OF THE DAYS OF OLD.

70 YEARS AGO.

" From Myles' Rambles in Forfarshire."

THE CROSS—HIGH STREET or MARKET PLACE IN THE OLDEN TIMES.

THE High Street, or Cross of Dundee, as it is commonly called, is a large rectangle, 360 feet long by 100 feet broad. No town in Scotland can boast of a more spacious centre, surrounded on all sides by commodious and elegant shops. No part of the town has undergone a more thorough change and reformation within the last 100 years than the Cross, and each successive change clearly shows the great improvement in taste and progress in wealth which the population have made in a single century. In 1746 there were not more than a dozen stone houses in the High Street. Most of the buildings were of wood; and the whole area lay in a state of filth which would not be tolerated at the present day. The " Shambles " or " Slaughter-House " occupied the site of the Trades Hall, at the top of Castle Street, and it was only in the end of the 18th century that the frightful nuisance was removed, and the Trades Hall erected on the spot. In the middle of the High Street stood the Market Cross which was re-constructed in 1586, and taken down in 1777. It was an octagonal erection, with six steps on each side, and the country women used to sit on the steps on Fridays, and sell their butter, cheese, and eggs. The fleshers in those days had stands on the High Street every Friday for the sale of beef. The only openings leading to the Shore were Tindal's Wynd, Couttie's Wynd, and the Vault. The Meal Market was held on the spot where the Old English Chapel or Union Hall stood, and in front of the Market there was a place called the "Tron," where salt was sold on market days and refractory soldiers were punished. The highest rent then drawn for a shop on the High Street was £3 per year; other shops could scarcely be let at any rent. From the improved and handsome shops very high rents are now drawn. "In those days," says a quaint writer already referred to, "the shopkeeper locked his door at one o'clock P.M., and retired to feed,—his customers were forced to wait his belly-filling, and there was no resource. Some of their shops contained a motley assortment of train oil and salt, candles and molasses, black soap and sugar, all crushed into less than a square of three or four yards." What would we moderns think of the character of a High Street shopkeeper who might now coolly lock his shop, put the key in his pocket, and walk off to dinner? The man would be consigned to a mad-house by his friends, and a more attentive and enterprising person would supplant him in his business. Competition has sharpened men's faculties, and given a great impetus during the last century to the industrial spirit. Every man must be active now; and if a shop-keeper has not enough to do to keep him active, he affects to be so. He knows that activity is the spirit of the age, and he fears that the public might conclude that he has too much spare time. Accordingly, young men in large shops are not allowed to sit— they must be active; and to keep them so—in appearance—they roll and unroll parcels, and are constantly working. The business habits of the last century would not answer our times. A century ago there was only a solitary one-horse chaise in Dundee, and now dozens stand at the stances alone, ready to be hired by the inhabitants. Great changes have taken place all over the town,

HIGH STREET—looking East—Seventy years ago.

but in no place are they more marked than at the Cross. From being a dirty area, enclosed by old wooden buildings, the ground flats of which were little superior to cobblers' stalls, it has now become a clean and favourite resort for loungers after business hours, and the buildings and shops which stand on every side are the most fashionable in town. At the Cross, on a fine summer evening, types of all classes and characters may be seen—from the learned lawyers down to a ragged club of unfortunates—and all of them present traits of social interest, and points for philosophical speculation.

In one corner may be seen standing a few venerable citizens—regular old stagers—whose gait, back and front, are as plain and palpable as the dial-plate of the town's clock. Like the Old Steeple or the Law, they are objects to be daily seen and all of them have been prominent characters of the town. They are in the yellow leaf of age, and they gather in a circle like a band of brothers who have long been separated, and are anxious to tell each other of their fortunes and misfortunes. They know all the affairs of the town; can tell you the name of every gentleman who passes, and something about his worldly prospects; know the salaries of all officials; and also who were Provost, Town Clerk, and even jailor, in 1801, and in all the other years in the century. They are lively and happy; and if at any time they indulge in lamentation, the theme of their wailings is the great degeneracy of the age, or the infinite and irreparable loss of "the good old times." They are, perhaps, members of the "Porter Club," or the "Toddy Club," or, perchance, of the "Welch Rabbit Club"—if of neither, they are, at all events, a *regular club*—they meet regularly—they talk regularly—they go away regularly—and in all their movements they are regular. If they indulge in a "parting glass" it must be a regular "tumbler," and taken at a regular house. In fact, you may as well think of pocketing the Custom House as of getting them to enter any new-fangled gaudy tavern. I like these old worthies—they are the living remains of the past century—the connecting link between a dead generation and a living. Their old contented countenances are like "holy places where happiness descending sits and smiles."

20

Here also may be seen another group ; they are young dandies —out and out fops ; they may be clerks, or juvenile haberdashers; they wear their hats in the oblique style of Paddy Weekes, carry a little cane in their right hands, and strut about from east to west, puffing the fumes of cigars in the faces of the passers-by. Draw near one of them—he is neat and clean, as if newly drawn from a " band-box," and he smells as if he carried a perfumer's shop in each pocket. On one finger he wears a huge gold ring, and a ponderous yellow chain dangles from his neck. His clothes are cut in the newest fashion, and so tight that he can scarcely turn and dare not bend. His mouth and chin look so mechanical and prim that one might imagine nature had made them for ornament rather than use. This young prig, in his own eyes, is refined, and speaks about the vulgar. Perhaps you will conclude that he is well-informed, and descended from some lucky mortal who has been " born with a silver spoon in his mouth." If you do you will be, as Sam Slick says, " tarnation wrong." Ask him a few questions in history, literature, or politics, and you will find that his mind is as barren as the " plain-stones." His father perchance is an honest and industrious man, who has worked hard, and made his son a gent ! and in return for his kindness, his son possibly does not know him on the street. It may be that the young " hopeful " sits behind a desk all day doing the mechanical drudgery of an office, and enjoys a salary nearly equal to the wages of a house-carpenter, and then comes out at night a regular swell member of " Young Dundee." When the tongue of the Old Steeple bell proclaims ten o'clock to the lieges, he, with his genteel friends, members of the " Puppy Club," shovel off to a fashionable tavern, call for " a go " of toddy, and kill time in sneering at female virtue, or in precocious talk on men, manners, and the fashions. A sorry crew are the " Puppy Club "—they ape the gentleman and play the fool—and, unfortunately for them, if experience teach them not wisdom, there is no " good time coming."

Look to some other corner, and you may see one standing alone. His clothes are shabby genteel, the hat encircled with a tattered piece of crape, his coat a misfit, out at the elbows, and

HIGH STREET—looking West—Seventy years ago.

too short in the sleeves ; the trousers, a light nankeen or faded black, thread-bare, patched at the knees, and fastened down by long leather straps ; his boots or shoes worn to shreds ; and his whole outward man characterized by the remains of a gentleman hanging on the skirts of a living beggar. This mortal possibly has seen better days. He has been unfortunate, or, as Cardinal Richlieu would have said, " he has been imprudent, for I do not understand what you mean by being unfortunate." He is a member of the " Victim Club." His brethren are numerous and united, but amongst them there is a fearful dearth of the " sinews of war." When they meet, if a shilling can be mustered, they co-operate in its " death." A coin of any description would " burn a hole in their pockets," and they rarely risk the experiment of detaining it. A member of the " Victim Club " is easily known. He stands very often at the corner of a street with his hands buried in his pockets, as if feeling for even the ghost of a penny, and he stares into vacancy as if haunted by the remembrance of better days. Poor fellow, perhaps he once kept a fine house, a horse and gig, drunk wine, and " turned over " hundreds of pounds a week, and dined with a few of his *dear* friends every Saturday. After dinner, the party, perhaps, resolved itself into a committee of " ways and means." concocted " wind bills," and, like drowning men, " caught at straws." But " time and tide will no man bide,"—all things come to an end, it is said, and our worthy came to his,—and there he stands, a picture of genteel misery and polite ragamuffinism. His old friends pass him with a cold look of contempt, and all avoid him as if he was a legal " scarecrow." The dignified *hauteur* of respectability, however, has no influence on the members of the " Victim Club." They are below the social lash, and they cannot feel its wounds. They can coolly pocket an affront, and as coolly ask you for the *loan* of a shilling. They are beyond the circle of society ; and morality and religion stand aghast when their reformation is contemplated. Alas ! poor victims, at times one of their number may be seen creeping about the Cross like a mouse seeking a morsel ; at other times he may be observed darting into a little shop in some obscure alley, then escaping from it with a halfpenny bannock in his hand, and hastily devouring it to allay the pressing pangs of hunger At the dawn of the day he may be seen stealing out from some "traveller's rest," creeping along the street until he meets another member of his club, from whom he begs a spark of the fire which *has burned* and will consume him. Besotted members of the "Victim Club," how miserable is your condition ! and, unfortunately, it is too often "past redemption."

In some other corner of the Cross may be seen a batch of social excrescences—out and out members of the "Ragamuffin Club." They are easily known, and carry the badge of their fraternity on their backs, and look as wretched as a starved Irishman clothed in his home-spun rags. "A fellow-feeling makes them wondrous kind " to each other, and they are crouching together in close consultation. They are "in the horrors." They have been all day on what they poetically denominate "the scuff", and are engaged cogitating on the gloomy state of their money market. Their expenditure, they find, has exhausted their funds, and the awful demon within still cries "Give ! give !" It is in vain. There is nothing to give, they have "perished the pack," and in rummaging their pockets they discover nothing but a few old tobacco pipes, and the dirty crumbs of farthing biscuits. What is to be done for the price of a gill ? They look at each other, feel their pipes with the points of their forefingers, but the very "dottles " are even gone—vanished into smoke, and they stand there literally "as poor as a church mouse." "Can we no raise threepence ?" asks one, in a state of despondency. There is no response, until one daring spirit, fit to be called the Chancellor of the Exchequer, steps forward and proposes a bold stroke of financial policy. He is the leader or a mouth-piece of the band, he can lead the members of his club through mazes of difficulties, until they land in the "Slough of Despond" of wretchedness. His scheme in such an emergency is simply to strip their shirts and consign them to their "uncle," on an advance of *one penny per shirt!* The proposition is consummated in the corner of a dark close. The needful is procured, and off they scamper to some unhallowed "howff" to swallow their shirt, and sing in character, as if mocking pale misery, "The

DUNDEE FROM THE STANNERGATE, 1822

cock may craw, the day may daw, but still we'll taste the barley bree." A common piece of business this is in the Ragamuffin Club. Its members are a lamentable crew—everlastingly grumbling at everybody and everything rather than at themselves; busy at all times in propagating misery, and multiplying paupers; steady only in one pursuit—doing evil. Look into one of their dingy whisky dens, and you will see one, perhaps, stretched on the floor drunk, and " driving his hogs to the market;" another, vomiting coarse and awful ribaldry; while a third, in true satiric style, demands order, and commences to recite—

> " How noble a creature is man—
> How exalted in reason, how infinite in faculties."

Suddenly the orator is interrupted in his unconscious burlesque, by his prostrate brother crying " That's a fact—bring in another gill." " There's nothing to pay it with," answers the spouter, in the exalted tone of recitation. " Get hing," responds the drowsy debauchee. " Pay on delivery is the order of this house," exclaims the landlord, as he walks into the room to turn them to the street, after he discovers they are destitute of the *wherewithal.* Infatuated mortals, doff the moral habiliments of the Ragamuffin Club, and become members of the Teetotal Club, and the change will be a blessed one for yourselves, your wives, and your families !

Here, again, is a large motley mob. They are collected at the south end of Reform Street, and visible at the Cross. They are composed of men, women, boys, and girls, young and old. According to a universal law they are in a circle. Some object of attraction is in the centre. What is it ? Why, it is our citizen minstrel—" Blind Hughie," with all the comic powers he can muster, singing—" We shall have a flare up." Having treated his audience to a tasting of broad humour, Hughie suddenly darts off into the inspiring and prophetic, and cheers his friends with the assurance that " There's a good time coming," if they will only have the good sense to " wait a little longer." It would have done Charles Mackay's heart good to hear Hughie chanting his " Good time coming." He does it with enthusiasm as if sympathising with the sentiments of the poet, and when he approaches its pithy lines, he glances to heaven, as if looking for inspiration, and he raises his voice to its utmost limits, until the very chimney-tops around reverberate with the sounds, and echo back—" Wait a little longer !" Hughie was one of our local characters, and a decent member of the " Griddler " profession. He was a married man, and had some stake in the country—as he was both a husband and father. Hughie first saw the light in the parish of Lauder, came to Dundee when a boy, almost lost his sight by disease ; and necessity, that heartless taskmaster, forced him to take to street singing. Not such a bad paying profession for Hughie. It was quite common for him to net 10s on a Saturday night ; and, be it remembered, he did not make a bad use of it—he was honest and temperate.

" BLIND HUGHIE."

IT is now nearly twenty years since Blind Hughie died. His real name was Hugh M. Gowans. As a wandering minstrel he enjoyed a widespread popularity, and nowhere was he a greater favourite than in Dundee. Hughie never used an instrument to accompany his vocal efforts, possibly he never learned to play one. His voice was his fortune, and his manner as he advanced in life became irresistibly grotesque and humorous. Any mimic who could hit off Hughie—and many tried it at concerts and social gatherings—was sure to convulse the audience with laughter. His stout burly figure stood as erect as a post. His hat thrown well back on his head showed his broad gaucy good-humoured face turned up to the sky. He always carried a walking stick, and when he began his entertainment he hung the staff by the crook over his left arm. Clearing his throat he struck up some favourite ditty in a voice rough and cracked, interrupted with a peculiar back draught as if he was short of breath. Added to that his body twisted in grotesque contortions, shrugging his shoulders, and hitching up his trousers as he caroled forth his songs in a style peculiarly his own. Comic singing was his *forte*, though he could with equal zest launch out into the sentimental and

BLIND HUGHIE.

From a Print.

LINDSAY STREET QUARRY.

Photo by Mr W. Bertie

patriotic field. "Stirling Bridge" was one of his favourite battle pieces, and he would roll out the stirring stanzas with such force and fire as to electrify his hearers. Some of his humorous ditties were not just rigidly moral in their composition, but they "took," and brought in the coppers, which was the main chance for Hughie. His favourite in the comic line was "Good News." It was a doggerel ditty descriptive of a shop stocked with a heterogeneous assortment of wares, from a needle to an anchor. The "pater" which Hughie rendered with great gusto never failed to tickle the risibilities of his audience. The articles on sale were given in ludicrous contrast—such as "Razor Straps and Curling Stanes, Epsom Salts and Wheelbarrows, Wine Grapes and Potatoe Graips, Masons' Mells and Gum Flowers, and Coarse Meal for Masons."

At feeing markets, fairs, and gatherings, Hughie was a prominent figure. He drew large crowds around him and earned plenty of money. As to his sobriety there was no question, and he was as honest as steel, and would have scorned to take a mean advantage of any one. One night, in Arbroath, the writer witnessed a pleasing illustration of Hughie's honesty. It was a Saturday night in the early autumn. The street lamps had not been fitted up for the winter months, and as it was growing late the streets were pretty dark. At the Tower Neuk, Hughie was rattling away in full glee, and had a closely packed circle of admirers around him. A poor woman squeezed herself into the crowd and slipped a coin into Hughie's hand. All at once he stopped in the middle of a verse and cried, " I say, mistress, that's a twa shilling piece you've gien me for a penny. Whaur are you." "Here Hughie, it was me," replied the woman quickly, " I thocht it was a penny." The honest fellow handed back the florin, and as ill luck would have it, the woman had no copper money in her possession. Thanking Hughie, she made an apology to that effect, "Never mind," returned Hughie. " You'll maybe hae a penny the next time I'm here." The crowd laughed, and cried " Well done Hughie," and coppers were showered in on him thick and fast.

Hughie was twice married. In the early years of his wedded

life he had a nice little home of his own in Kirriemuir to which he returned for rest after his professional wanderings. Evil days fell on the poor man. His wife was a native of Montrose, and induced by her desire to be near her own people Hughie removed his headquarters to that town. Misfortune overtook him. His wife fell into bad health, the house was broken up, and Hughie had to take up his abode in a common lodging house. From Montrose he itinerated around the towns in Forfarshire, Brechin and Forfar being his favourite resorts, where he was well known and very popular. Occasionally he travelled over the Mearns, frequently visited the Granite City and went beyond it to the far North.

Hughie's wife died in the Montrose Infirmary. The funeral was grotesquely described in one of the local newspapers. The only mourners were Hughie, the bereaved husband, and Willie Gunn, another half blind man who made a living by selling almanacs on the streets in winter, and dealing in old books in summer. The coffin was placed in a small mean-looking hearse. Hughie took hold of the vehicle at the back, Willie linked into Hughie's arm, and off the cortège started. The wag of a driver put his horse to a good trot, and the ludicrous spectacle of two blind men holding on to the rear of a hearse and running as hard as they could created quite a scene on the streets.

In the later years of his life Hughie located himself in Dundee, making short tours to the neighbouring towns. When at home he was a regular attender at the sittings of the Police and Sheriff Courts. He fell into bad health and died in very poor circumstances.

i

From a Print.

CHURCHES BEFORE THE FIRE.

Photo by Mr W. Bertie.

27

A NORTHERN PUBLISHER.

Reprinted from " The Traveller," Glasgow, July 4, 1885.

DUNDEE has improved so much and so rapidly of late that it is impossible to tell—assuming it keeps on improving at the same ratio—to what eminence it may rise in the future. It began with jute, but what it will end in is a matter for speculation. Personally, we have the greatest love for the historic northern town, and we view with interest every step it takes toward advancement.

Much of this, however, we have from time to time noticed, has been the work of prominent citizens and business men, and we could point to not a few gentlemen whose names are destined to be honoured ones in the town records. Mr Alexander Maxwell, in his recent admirable history of Dundee, and Mr C. C. Maxwell, in his article in the " Encyclopædia Britannica," have shown how far a town can progress under careful management, and by the generosity of wealthy inhabitants. Thus from a small sea-port town of comparative insignificance, it has risen to the dignity of being the third town in Scotland in point of population, and second in commercial importance.

With that, however, in the meantime, we have little to do, our intention, at present, being to point briefly to a gentleman well-known and respected in the town of which he is a citizen.

Mr William Kidd, Dundee, is a name familiar to every one interested in publishing and printing north of the Forth. His life, like that of the good town he lives in, has been a series of improvements and successes from the time (to say nothing of his earlier life as assistant to Mr Shaw for over 20 years, whose business he afterwards bought) he opened a " wee " shop in Union Street on "his ain accoont" to the present, when he has built for himself the handsome block of buildings in Whitehall Street. To note the successive steps leading up to this, the latest of his enterprises, would be doubtless very interesting reading, but Mr Kidd would be the last, we are sure, to consent to such a thing. Let it suffice, then, to indicate merely that his life has been a hard working one, early at his post in the morning, and " late at e'en " before his self-allotted tasks were accomplished. Viewed in the light of these facts, there is considerable truth in the apt conceit recently made by a local gentleman on the occasion of the opening of Mr Kidd's new premises—the Whitehall Palace Buildings. " It was," said the gentleman referred to, " mentioned in the Bible ' that men who were diligent in business would stand before kings ' ; but Mr Kidd had gone a step beyond that, for he was now in the Palace itself."

Before we refer more minutely to the new premises in White- hall Street, it will be necessary to indicate to the reader certain particulars concerning the street itself. First of all, it is a new street, formed only a few years ago by the removal of some of the oldest property in Dundee. It runs from the Nethergate down to West Dock Street, taking a bold curve at the bottom. In every sense it is an improvement, and when all the buildings shall have been erected it will be one of the most popular thoroughfares—in fact, the Regent Street of Dundee. The removal of the old Union Hall, which blocked the entry to the Nethergate, was the signal for the demolition of the series of closes and old houses which seemed to bear it company. Few people, unless antiquarians, will regret their destruction, however ; and the younger generation will rejoice in the glory of the modern architecture which is now taking their place.

Yet, for a long time, this desirable thoroughfare obtained scant welcome ; indeed, as far as we can remember, there was some very noisy disputes concerning it. It stood long, therefore, mutely pathetic, imploring, by means of an array of notice boards, enter- prising men to step in and feu it. It is to the honour of Mr Kidd that he was the first to break the ice of cold indifference by taking a stance in the new street. For this enterprise the people of Dundee should be greatly indebted to him.

The stance taken, Mr Kidd commissioned his friend Mr Keith,

WHITEHALL STREET. *Kidd's Whitehall Palace Buildings.*

the well-known architect, to prepare plans, with the result that on the 27th March last the first building in Whitehall Street was inaugurated.

The style of the building, which has been justly christened the "Palace Buildings," is ornamental Gothic, and is of very handsome appearance, as will be judged from the sketch we have made of it.

The two shops are splendidly fitted up and lighted, the saloons being each about 26 feet by 32 feet, and the front shops 40 feet by 30 feet. The sides are built in piers, which is of great utility for cases and shelving; and all the window fittings are of mahogany. From the shop, which Mr Kidd is to occupy himself, is an elegant stairway leading to the flat above, which is to be the resting place of the University Club. For this purpose, therefore, the flat has been arranged as library and reading-room, with lavatories, etc. The second shop, when we visited it, was occupied by a Fine Art Exhibition, and it struck us that no place could have been found more suitable as to light and space.

The elevation at back, which consists of Mr Kidd's workshops, etc., is of four storeys. The basement floor is the machine-room, and for that purpose it is admirably adapted, being very commodious. A six H.P. " Otto " engine provides the motive power. The second floor is devoted to lithographic work, of which Mr Kidd is justly famous, his productions being in every respect artistic and well finished. The third floor is set apart as the binding-room, and here may be seen all the modern apparatus necessary in the art of bookbinding. The fourth floor is the composing-room, being in every respect well constituted for such a purpose— that most precious thing for the compositor—light—being well diffused throughout. Piercing all these floors is a powerful hoist, which gives great facility for the expeditious removal of heavy articles. It stands to reason, therefore, that Mr Kidd is now more in a position than ever to execute very large commissions, whether these consist in publishing, printing, lithographing, bookbinding, or bookselling.

Three minutes' walk from the Palace Buildings, brings us to Mr Kidd's old shop, which was the University College Warehouse of

30

Dundee, just as Mr Thin's of Edinburgh, and Maclehose's of Glasgow, are the respective shops where University men of these towns love to congregate. Within the limited space in that same little establishment of which we are speaking, we have at times seen gathered most of the literary and professional gentlemen of Dundee. Prominent among these may have been seen the tall, spare form of a leading legal and literary "light," or the burly person of the latest historian of Dundee, or the active, sharp figure of an antiquarian, or—well these will do at present; we will leave all that for another day to accomplish. It is all very interesting, however, and we are sure none of our readers are so sorry as ourselves that our space compels us, all too soon, to close our remarks. Let us hope that at no very distant date we may once again take up the thread of our discourse with more time and space at our command. Of the books published by Mr Kidd we may mention "The History of Old Dundee," by Alex. Maxwell; "The Gilfillan Birth-day Book," "The Art of Weaving Linen and Jute Manufactures by Power Loom," and his famous county map of Forfar divided into parishes.

THE WISHART ARCH

SALE SHOP.

31

EXTRACTED FROM—

"Scotland Up to Date," 1898.

FOR generations past Scotland has been noted for the number and importance of its publishing houses, although hitherto these have been generally confined to the capital or to Glasgow. There has been, however, no reason for this limitation ; and that such businesses can flourish equally well in other centres of population, the successful career of the house of Mr William Kidd, of Dundee, abundantly demonstrates. Mr Kidd has made for himself a leading reputation in the printing and publishing trades in Scotland ; and his experience should encourage others to start similar establishments, which may become the head-quarters of literary activity in various localities, and incentives to the study of local antiquities and history. It is now over a quarter of a century since Mr Kidd commenced business, at first on comparatively modest lines, in Dundee. His original premises were in Union Street, but these soon proved too confined to meet the exigencies of an ever-increasing business, and a removal was made to Nethergate, with a like result. With characteristic enterprise Mr Kidd then purchased a large space in Whitehall Street, and erected the handsome Palace Buildings, which he now occupies. These have an imposing facade, and are four storeys in height, with a spacious basement. The latter is utilised for the machining room, stereotyping room and store, and is as complete as modern printing engineering skill can render it. All of the newest and best machines are in use : Wharfedale, Arab, and Pearl (12 in number), also paper cutting machine, power being obtained from a fine large sized "Otto" gas engine. This department presents, at all times, a scene of great activity. On the ground floor is the general retail shop, which is very commodious and admirably arranged, containing a very large and well-selected stock of Books, plain and fancy stationery of all descriptions, and every requisite for the office, schoolroom and study. We also noticed a splendid collection of Bibles, prayer books, Church services and hymnals, in a great variety of choice bindings ; tourist writing-cases, photo and scrap albums, writing desks and inkstands, despatch boxes, pocket books, purses, letter cases, card cases, etc., etc., in all the newest and best styles. Artists, amateur and professional, will find here all the requisites for their craft, including materials by the most famous manufacturers. On the same floor as the shop is the lending library, which is equipped with over 7,000 volumes, including all the latest and most popular novels and standard works, by the most eminent authors. New books are being continually added, and this is certainly the most complete establishment of the kind north of the Forth.

The works published by Mr William Kidd form in themselves a formidable library. His interesting and beautifully illustrated series of Guides to Dundee and District are well-known to all tourists in the east of Scotland, and are valuable additions to the typographical works dealing with this historic district. He has also published books dealing with local industries and the social condition of the workers, religious works, medical works, and hand-books to various examinations. Being himself an antiquary and historical student of no mean pretensions, Mr Kidd devotes great attention to works dealing with these subjects, and several books published by him, in this department, are regarded as of standard character : the following are the Titles of a few :—

ANCIENT DUNDEE—Illustrated—Demy oblong, 4to. (in the Press).

ALEX. MAXWELL'S OLD DUNDEE—Ecclesiastical, Burghal, and Social, prior to the Reformation.

    Do.   do.   The History of Old Dundee after the Reformation.

W. LEGGATT'S THEORY AND PRACTICE OF JUTE SPINNING — With Illustrations of the various Machines.

    Do.   THE ART OF WEAVING, 2 vols.

    Do.   STUDENT'S EDITION OF ART OF WEAVING, 1 vol.

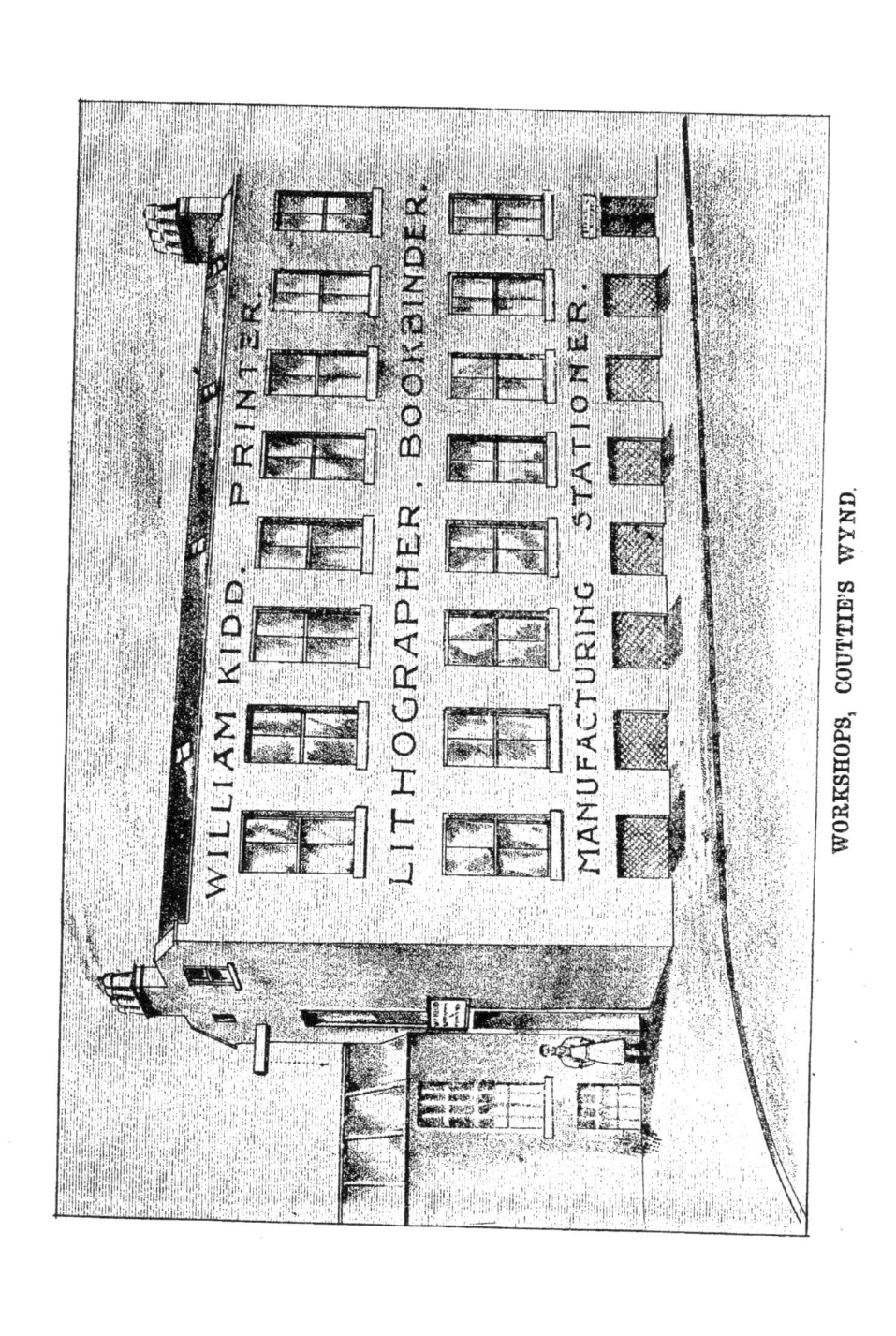

WORKSHOPS, COUTTIE'S WYND.

Rev. W. B. Inglis' Beloved for their Works' Sake.

Rev. R. Waterson's Thoughts on the Lord's Supper

Life of a Dundee Draper.

D. M. Nicoll's Character Sketches.

Chapter in the Life of a Dundee Factory Boy.

William Hay's Ancient Dundee.

Extracts from Records of the Presbytery of Brechin, 1639-1660.

Foo Foozle and His Friends.

The Chartists' Agitation in Dundee.

Dundee Press Roll—(in the Press.)

Schussler's Abridged Therapeutic, edited by Mrs Walker
    Do.   Cure of Diphtheria,   do.   do.

Domestic Guide to the use of Schussler's Remedies

Rev. John Wallace's Expositions of Christian Doctrines.

Dr. Pirie's Notes on Health.

Dr. M'Nutt's Asthma, Is it Curable?

A. Paul's Random Readings.

Ross Campbell's Humorous Irish Sketches.

Capt. Wood's New Edition of Allen's Guide to Mates and Masters.

Allen's Extra Master's Guide.

Gilfillan Birthday Book.
    Do.   Five Discourses, 1837—(Reprint.)

Rev. W. Walsh's Lecture on Gilfillan.

A Series of Excursions for 20 Miles around Dundee

Guide to Dundee.
    Do.   do.   From the Tramway Cars.
    Do.   to Arbroath.
    Do.   to the Rivers Tay and Earn.

City Songs by Norval Scrymgeour.

Maggie Aimer's Blue Ribbon.

Rev. Dr. Dunlop's Genuine and Spurious Protestantism

Papers Read before the Association of Office-bearers of the Church of Scotland.

In Remembrance of Rev. Thos. B. Dodds.

William H. Blakeney's Continuous Railway Brakes.

Large Wall Map of Forfarshire.

Handy Pocket Map of Perthshire.

RANDOM SKETCHES—H.M.S. PINAFORE.
UNIVERSITY COLLEGE MAGAZINE.
DUNDEE INSTITUTION ANNUALS.
Do.　HARRIS ACADEMY ANNUALS.
Do.　HIGH SCHOOL MAGAZINE (Monthly).
CONSTITUTION HOUSE MAGAZINE.
GRAPHIC ARTS ANNUALS.
PIPER O' DUNDEE—(First Issue, 1877.)
OUR SPECIAL ARTIST AT EXHIBITION, 1877—3 Visits.
ETC., ETC , ETC.

On the same floor, passing) through the shop, we come to the store, stock rooms, and the lithographic room, the latter containing presses, cutting machines, etc., in fact all the requisite machinery for the prompt execution of orders in memoranda, invoices, letter-headings, visiting, invitation, and menu cards, marriage and " at home " cards, architects' plans and specifications, circulars in plain and ornamental writing, etc. In this branch very artistic work is produced on the shortest notice. On the floor above is the composing room, 75 feet in length. It is equipped with an almost endless variety of founts of types. In this department only thoroughly experienced hands are employed, and all orders are executed on the shortest notice, in a style displaying expert and finished workmanship in every detail. On the top floor book-binding, die-stamping, and paper-ruling— American Striker and two Hand String machines—are carried on ; and we may mention that Mr Kidd has the largest book-binding plant (out of Edinburgh and Glasgow) in Scotland. We were much struck by the excellent ventilation of the whole establishment, and were convinced that all operations were being carried on under perfect sanitary conditions. The business is admirably managed and organised throughout, and reflects the highest credit upon its enterprising and energetic principal, who finds employment for sixty-five hands. Mr Kidd is well known throughout the publishing trade, and in literary circles. His unfailing courtesy and uprightness of character have gained him universal esteem, and all will wish him a continuance of that prosperity which his career has so fully merited.

THE "BLUE BELL."

The "Blue Bell" Tavern stood at the top of Seagate, and was a favourite public resort, especially by country people on market days for "pies and porter." The pies were supplied by Smith, the famous pie baker, in the small shop adjoining the entrance to the tavern.

THE METHODIST CHURCH, OVERGATE (Old).

EXTRACTED FROM—

" Evening Telegraph," Xmas, 1900.

NOVELTIES AT MR W. KIDD'S WHITEHALL STREET.

There appears to be a feeling for highly-coloured Christmas cards this season, but Mr Kidd, I think, has wisely elected to remain faithful to the artistic black and white, sepia and softly tinted cards with which we have been familiar for many years now. Nothing very striking is to be noticed this year, unless "The Dundee Souvenir"—a tiny booklet in parchment cover, containing some half-dozen views, of city streets and buildings, by Valentine. The calendars are as charming as ever The sporting series is likely to appeal to the taste of the sterner sex, whilst the floral specimens are dainty enough to adorn " my lady's boudoir." The children's toy and picture books deserve a special notice all to themselves, but want of space forbids, and I must only refer to the amusing " Dumpy books " in diminutive form, excellent type, and coloured pictures ; to books, combining song, story, and music ; and to a very attractive volume, " A Trip to Toyland," with most comical illustrations. By the way, I noticed a series of 6d cartoons, needless to add of a highly humorous nature, by Cynicus, who is also responsible for not a few of the funniest Xmas cards. Delightful gifts for friends abroad other than cards with sprigs of heather, are the neat, little, tartan-covered books at 6d each, with Burns' or Scott's poems, or " Rob Roy," or an attractive volume of " National Melodies " with music complete. The new century Thackeray of 14 volumes in beautiful case, costing only two guineas, suggests itself as a handsome present for a book-lover. Mrs Gaskell's popularity is evinced by an excellent edition of her works, enclosed in a strong, neat case, and one can't help wondering if the enthusiastic interest re-awakened in the Brontës accounts for this fact. George Eliot's complete works, similarily got up, are priced at £2 7s 6d, and there is a companion set of Shakespeare in handy red-bound volumes. Dr. J. R. Miller is represented by a dainty volume in Pale Blue and White Binding —"Golden Gates of Prayer"—and a lovely Christmas booklet; whilst the Rev. F. B. Meyer's new book—"Love, Courtship, and Marriage"—is displayed. Devotional books are noticeable in great variety. "Five Minutes" gives extracts from the finest poems, and a Book of Common Prayer may be had in a slightly elongated style, a little larger and thicker than a good sized purse. A remarkably good edition of Scott, with something like 200 steel engravings by famous artists, is presently being offered at five guineas, which is simply half the usual price. The latest books and novels are, of course, displayed here, including "Helen Faucit" and "The Life of the Earl of Rosebery." In games, "Patience" more than holds its own still, and there is a new game, "Wheeling," which purports to be a winter game for cyclists! A suitable gift for wheel men and women would be one of the pretty red morocco-bound "Rambles on Wheels," in which they may record the date of their runs and any other information. An "At Home" book in the same style would prove acceptable to the lady with a long visiting list and a short memory! Nice whist markers at 1s a pair commend themselves to card players, as well as the packs and boxes of bezique, &c. Writing albums, of which there are some lovely specimens, are supposed to come specially within the province of young ladyhood, just as compact pocket-books belong exclusively to the masculine mind. Little gilt stamp holders, with the Queen depicted on one side and Rowland Hill on the other, are as novel as useful, and cheap at 3d. "Tuck" purses of sealskin prepared in Dundee are likely to find favour with those who fancy a soft, handy purse, which will not speedily give way although constantly in use. Photo frames in various styles and sizes, albums, dressing-cases and bags, stationery cabinets and writing folios, are to be noted, and all are marked by the substantiality and good taste characteristic of Mr Kidd's old-established business.

DESIGNED, PRINTED, AND LITHOGRAPHED ON THE PREMISES.